"Dear Parents and Caregivers,
This book is designed to nurture both the hearts of children and the understanding of the adults who love them. Most children come to Earth with unique spiritual gifts—this story is here to celebrate those gifts and inspire you to see the magic in your child" and inspire your child to see the magic in themselves!

"To the beautiful children
who see beyond the stars,
and the parents who guide
them with love.
This book is for you."

Siena often felt like she didn't quite belong.
She could feel things others didn't notice, like the sadness in a friend's smile or the joy hiding in the song of birds.
Sometimes, she even saw colours around people, soft glows that changed with their moods.

But when she tried to explain it, others would just smile and say, "You've got such a big imagination!"
Siena looked up at the stars and whispered,
"Why do I feel so different and sometimes like I don't belong here?"

"Hello, Siena," came a voice as soft as moonlight. Siena turned to see a glowing figure standing by her window. The figure's light blended with the stars, making them almost part of the sky. "Who…who are you?" Siena asked, her heart racing but her fear melting under the figure's gentle smile.

"I am your guide," the being said. "I've come to remind you of something you've always known but have forgotten. You are made of stardust."

Siena blinked. "Stardust? Like…the stars?"

"Exactly like the stars," the guide replied. "And just like the stars, you shine in your own unique way."

The guide held out her hand, and suddenly Siena was no longer in her room. She was among the stars, her body glowing like a little star herself. "Every part of you," the guide explained, "is connected to this universe. Your feelings, your gifts, your light, they all come from the stars and planets in the cosmos."
They flew past a glowing nebula, where stars were being born.

"See this? Just like the stars, you were created to shine in your own way." Siena looked at her hands, which sparkled with stardust.

"But why do I feel so different?"

"Because your gifts make you special," the guide said. "You feel deeply, and you notice things others might not. That's your light—it's how you help the world see beauty and kindness."

"Will people ever understand me?" Siena asked softly.
"Some will," the guide replied, "and some won't. But that doesn't change who you are. Your light is yours to share with the world. The right people will see it, and they will love you for it."
Siena smiled, her heart feeling warm and bright. She wasn't just different, she was special.
And she would never forget it.

As Siena drifted off to sleep,
she whispered to the stars,
"Thank you."
And in the distance, it felt
like the stars were
whispering back to her,
"Shine, little one. Shine."

The Magic of Starseed Children

Some children seem to carry a special light—like they've come to Earth with a deeper purpose.
These are Starseed children.
Believed to have souls from the stars, they're here to help the world heal and grow during a time of transformation.
They bring powerful gifts:
✨ Deep intuition and sensitivity to unseen energy
✨ Natural kindness and empathy
✨ Bright ideas to inspire a better future

The Different Types of Starseed Souls

As the ascension unfolds, many types of Starseed souls are arriving on Earth, each with their own mission and light.

Indigo Children

Bold and determined, Indigo Children are natural leaders and system-breakers. They challenge outdated ways of thinking and create space for fairness, freedom, and truth.

Crystal Children

Peaceful and deeply compassionate, Crystal Children radiate unconditional love. They help bring harmony and teach the world about forgiveness and unity.

Rainbow Children
Joyful and creative, Rainbow Children radiate positivity and remind us of life's magic, helping to heal with their light energy.

Diamond Children
Rare and radiant, Diamond Children hold pure, high-frequency energy. They anchor divine light and inspire deeper spiritual connection.

Old Souls
Wise beyond their years, Old Souls carry ancient wisdom and feel deeply connected to the stars, Earth, and universal truths.

Next book in the series will explore more.....

Nurturing Your Child's Intuitive Gifts

Spiritually aware, sensitive, and intuitive children thrive when they feel seen, heard, and safe to express who they are.

Here's how you can support their journey:

🌟 **Listen with an Open Heart**

When your child shares a dream, feeling, or a unique experience, meet them with curiosity—not correction.

Try asking:

💬 "How did that make you feel?"

💬 "Did it feel exciting, comforting, or maybe a little strange?"

💬 "Would you like to draw or talk more about it?"

These small moments of acceptance help them feel empowered to trust their inner world.

Validate Their Experiences

Let your child know that their gifts are real and special, even if others may not understand.
Phrases like "That sounds amazing," or "You have such a wonderful way of seeing the world," can make them feel valued and understood.

Create a Safe Environment for Exploration

Provide tools to help them express themselves, such as, Journals for writing down their dreams or feelings.
Crystals, drawing supplies, or calming objects to help them connect with their energy.

Understanding Starseed Children's Emotions

Starseed children feel emotions deeply. Their heightened sensitivity allows them to connect with others on a profound level, often sensing feelings that aren't spoken aloud. While this is a beautiful gift, it can sometimes feel overwhelming.

Empathy ~ They absorb the energy of people and places, which can make them feel others' joys and struggles as if they were their own.

Emotional Intensity ~Their emotions are often powerful and may come in waves, requiring gentle guidance to process them.

Teach Them to Set Boundaries and Protection.
Sensitive children can sometimes feel overwhelmed by energy.
Teach them to ~ Say "no" if they feel uncomfortable.
Setting intentions to call back their own energy and give back any energy that have taken from others back.
Visualize a protective bubble of white light around themselves or they can ask their spirit guides or angels to surround them with protection daily or as needed.
Let them choose a crystal for protection to carry around with them. But make sure the crystal is cleansed regularly.
Regularly cleanse your home with smudge.

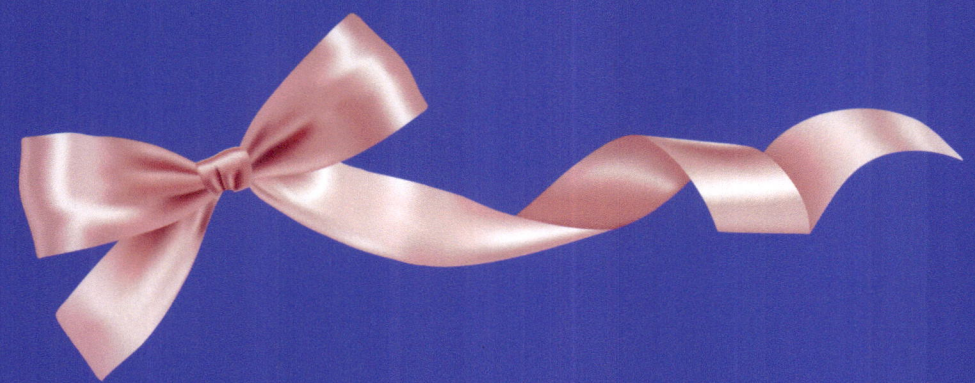

A Loving Reminder

You are your child's greatest guide. By offering love, understanding, and encouragement, you help them embrace their gifts and step into their light with confidence and joy.

Author Teane Kenny is a spiritual mentor, healer, and teacher whose soul origins are among the stars. With a deep calling to support Starseed children and their families, her work is focused on helping them embrace their gifts and navigate their unique journeys.

She specialises in:

✨ Guiding families and individuals through the ascension process

✨ Energy healing and intuitive support

✨ Helping children manage sensitivity and emotional overwhelm

✨ Nurturing spiritual gifts with love and purpose

If you or your child need guidance, Teane offers sessions both in person and remotely—creating a safe, supportive space where your child can truly thrive.

For more information or to book an appointment, please contact
Teane via her website
www.shamanicdreaming.org